FAMILY HOUSES
in the COUNTRY

FAMILY HOUSES
in the COUNTRY

ALEXANDRA D'ARNOUX
GILLES DE CHABANEIX

Translated by Paul Stuart Rankin

CLARKSON POTTER/PUBLISHERS
NEW YORK

Published by Clarkson Potter/Publishers, 201 East 50th Street, New York, New York 10022.
Member of the Crown Publishing Group.

Random House, Inc. New York, Toronto, London, Sydney, Auckland
www.randomhouse.com

Clarkson N. Potter, Potter, and colophon are registered trademarks of Random House, Inc.

Printed in China

Design by Frauke Famira

Library of Congress Cataloging-in-Publication Data
Arnoux, Alexandra d'.
    Family houses in the country / Alexandra d'Arnoux and Gilles de Chabaneix ; translated by
Paul Stuart Rankin. — 1st ed.
    1. Vacation homes—Europe Pictorial works. 2. Vacation homes—United States Pictorial works.
3. Interior decoration—Europe—History—20th century Pictorial works. 4. Interior decoration—United
States—History—20th century Pictorial works. 5. Lifestyles—Europe—History—20th century Pictorial works.
6. Lifestyles—United States—History—20th century Pictorial works. I. De Chabaneix, Gilles. II. Title.
NK2195.V34A76   2000
909'.09734—dc21   99-36149
                                                                                CIP

ISBN 0-517-70860-4
10 9 8 7 6 5 4 3 2 1
First Edition

To Victor and Alexandre, with love.

ALEXANDRA D'ARNOUX

To Catherine, my wife.

GILLES DE CHABANEIX

ACKNOWLEDGMENTS

The authors and the publisher wish to thank all those who have permitted their houses to be included in this book, houses that so beautifully exemplify the spirit of family.

Victor et Alexandre Labarthe d'Arnoux

Mr. and Mrs. Peter Calender Beckett

Comte et Comtesse Jean-Marc de la Bédoyère

Madame Thérèse de la Bédoyère

Mr. and Mrs. R. O. Blechman

Monsieur et Madame Joseph de Boisanger

Madame Lorraine de Boisanger

Monsieur et Madame Lorenzo Borletti

Monsieur et Madame Guy Boucher

Madame Brigitte Bourbigot

Mrs. Emma Bridgewater and
  Mr. Matthew Rice

Comtesse de las Cases

Catherine de Chabaneix

Martin et Simon de Chabaneix

Mr. and Mrs. Don Chappellet

Monsieur et Madame Bernard Cohen

Madame Nicole Deschars

Mr. and Mrs. Thomas Escher

Comte et Comtesse Hubert de
  Roquemaurel Galitzine

Mr. and Mrs. Amaury de Grandmaison

Mrs. Sally Griffiths

Marquis et Marquise d'Hemery

Monsieur et Madame Philippe Labro

Monsieur Bruno de Laubadère

Mr. and Mrs. Fritz Link

Comte et Comtesse Armand Ghislain
  de Maigret

Mr. and Mrs. Alexander McEwan

Mr. John McLane

Monsieur et Madame Jean-Louis Mellerio

Monsieur et Madame Olivier Mellerio

Monsieur et Madame Michel Meneur

Mr. and Mrs. Scott Moreau

Mrs. Monina von Opel and
  Mr. Edward F. Miller

Madame Catherine Painvin

Ralph Lauren Co.

Monsieur Robert de Rothschild

Mr. and Mrs. Elie Sehnaoui

Mr. and Mrs. David Stewart

Mr. and Mrs. Walter Sullivan

Monsieur et Madame Ben Swildens

Monsieur et Madame Gilles Tronel

Voyageurs du Monde—Madame Eve Baume

CONTENTS

The Spirit of Family

We each carry within us the image of a beloved house.
A marvelous family house, an expansive memory catcher.
I was still rather young, and we ate our meals in the children's
dining room. How well I remember that room. On the ground were
beautiful lustrous brick-red tiles, on the walls English engravings
so familiar that one no longer saw them. But each day as we sat at
table we did admire the collection of porcelain *trompe l'oeils,* which
in our eyes were worth all earthly nourishment. Arranged on a
sideboard were brown walnuts with exquisite detailing, a fake
nutcracker, bright lemons placed on shiny leaves, and peas—much
larger and prettier than real ones. And eggs. Unlike the ones that
were served to us, these seemed unbreakable, which filled us with
joy. We spoke of "hard-boiled eggs" with the ecstatic laughter of
children sharing a joke beyond the comprehension of adults.

I returned to that dining room a year ago. Nothing had changed.
The *trompe l'oeils* were still in their place, as was the big black piano
against the rear wall. Only the children eating their snacks about
the round mahogany table were different. Yet they resembled us
prodigiously. Little nephews, little cousins . . . their laughter, just like
ours, erased the barrier of time and returned to me a bit of my
vanished childhood.

Unimportant details? On the contrary, very important details, for
family houses are built around these essential little nothings that erect
a delicate footbridge between generations.

Very slowly, let us open a first door and enter quietly.

COUNTRY LIVING

Bardochat, a vast dwelling with Victorian accents, was built by Alexander's grandfather over one hundred years ago. OVERLEAF *Wonderful iron fences run over the hills capturing bits of rolling green fields.*

This afternoon the salon is flooded with light. It streams in through two large bay windows that open onto an immense expanse of lawn. Outside, the trees are haloed by a soft green mist. Tufts of daffodils appear in the grass. In spite of a good early spring sun, a blazing fire crackles in the fireplace. Alexander seems a bit squeezed between the arms of his favorite armchair. From time to time he interrupts his reading and his sober, almost hollow voice resembles the rolling of benevolent thunder as he turns toward Cecilia.

Cecilia, wrapped in an immense apron and completely absorbed, puts the final touches on a collage. The table over which she is leaning almost completely disappears under a carpet of paper petals which she cuts out with precision.

14

Stretched out on the carpet, Bella, one of the family dogs, warms her bones without losing a bit of the scene, although she pretends to sleep. She wouldn't want to miss a walk!

The winter months seem very far off—those terrible months when masses of black clouds go scudding across the sky, when the rain crashes violently down against the house, ceaselessly, without respite. Those months when one lives barricaded behind closed shutters, when the wind from the Atlantic howls down the chimneys.

"Our friends find those times romantic; I find them terrifying," says Cecilia. "My children, for as long as we have lived here, do not understand why I insist on staying in my room—which reverberates with a frightful uproar when it is hit by a storm. But I cannot leave it, I would always be missing something. And then I don't want to, especially because of the dogs who sleep, one on my bed and the other at the foot, and who hate to be disturbed."

Whether it rains, whether the wind blows, or whether the sun suddenly lights up the countryside, Bardochat is worthy of appearing in one of those marvelous films that make us nostalgic for the past.

Built in 1896 by the celebrated Scottish architect Robert Lorimer, Bardochat towers over the valley of Stinchar, an idyllic landscape, a mixture of hills and dales strewn with sheep so white they appear to be made of porcelain. In the beginning it was a hunting lodge where Alexander's grandfather shot grouse. It welcomed his hunting friends, their wives, and at least as many servants. Travel at that time was no mean feat. One did not settle in for just a weekend, so there was no question of leaving anything behind—especially not one's valet or chambermaid!

Alexander remembers the Bardochat of his childhood as a hospitable house, full of people, rustling with comings and goings, where conversations flowed at a great pace, where one lived well

OPPOSITE AND ABOVE *Very early each morning, while the household is still dozing, Alexander will descend the stairs and stop for an instant in the pine-paneled hallway to check the time by the big clock.* OVERLEAF *The welcome disorder of the small salon.*

19

under all circumstances . . . even during the Second World War.

"I was five years old," he remembers. "We had been evacuated here. My grandfather was no longer living but my grandmother was still with us. The house was packed. We were seven children, my aunt had six. I still wonder how we managed to fit as there was, in addition to the family, a whole parallel universe of cooks, chambermaids, and nannies. The children were lodged at the back of the house on the top floor in three nurseries turned into dormitories. Here we occupied a world apart. Nanny's room was just next door to ours. A kind of cat's hole or pass-through was dug into the wall between the two rooms. From time to time, Nanny would raise the little trapdoor to make sure that her charges were still sleeping soundly. Thus, she could watch over our sleep from her armchair."

OPPOSITE *The dining room was stenciled by Emily Todhunter.* TOP *Two portraits by Lazlo, of Alexander's father and uncle, contemplate the peaceful scene in the living room.* ABOVE *Alexander in his favorite chair.*

23

ABOVE RIGHT *There is no family house without family photos in good order on the piano.* RIGHT *A backgammon set, finely embroidered by an expert hand.* OPPOSITE *A portrait by Lavery of Alexander's grandmother with her two daughters dominates the music room.*

24

As long as nurseries have existed, they have been located apart from the rest of the house. The children grew up in a bell jar until the age of ten or twelve, like solid little shrubs in a greenhouse. The rules of good breeding were inculcated there. One was punished, scolded, cajoled by nannies. The sole masters on board, they regulated the lives of the children over whom they reigned like metronomes. In retrospect, this seems extraordinarily reassuring, for one was protected from everything, left to be busy with growing up.

Children lunched and dined separately, with their Nanny, in the children's dining room, and were sent outside in all kinds of weather. And every evening before going to bed they would each sit beside a Miss Nightingale, all fresh and clean in their little pajamas, well wedged in against her. She then read a chapter—and no more, it was

ABOVE *Brass beds, dressing tables, eclectic associations of furniture and of memories accumulated over generations . . . upstairs, bedrooms and bathrooms open onto endless corridors.* OPPOSITE *Collections of opaline glass, of toilet articles—the charm of the past.*

26

useless to insist—of *The Wind in the Willows*. Then she would shut her book and give a kiss to send her charges off to bed.

Incursions into the lives of parents took place at fixed times. At a precise moment one was brought in to say good morning. Very neat, with clean hands and straight parts in their hair, the little ones climbed the stairs, moved slowly down the corridor, and knocked on their parents' bedroom door, entering quietly, slightly intimidated, as good as gold. "Mother would be finishing her breakfast, so beautiful in her baldachin bed, leaning against little lace pillows, that I hardly dared sit on her comforter."

In a world that is ceaselessly changing, family houses embody continuity through so many shared memories. Fishing parties on the Stinchar River—an echo of the hunts of old—reunite young and old,

27

ABOVE *Cecilia in riding dress.*
RIGHT *A stone staircase leads
to the woods.* OPPOSITE
*Spring has barely dawned in
the garden where Cecilia
spends long hours.* OVERLEAF
*An impressive feature of the
gardens at Bardochat are these
huge expanses of lawns that
carry the eye toward the hills
and the sea beyond. One can
almost hear the sea break.*

as do picnics on the moors. And as do certain considerations that
one does not forget. At Bardochat, when one goes to bed, instead of
finding oneself in the darkness of one's room, one finds that the
stoves have been comfortably purring for hours, a friendly hand has lit
the bedside lights, and the beds, open to sheets of heavy white cotton
embroidered with initials in arabesques, are an invitation to dream.

One has sweet dreams at Bardochat.

THE SECRETS OF BAGNOLI

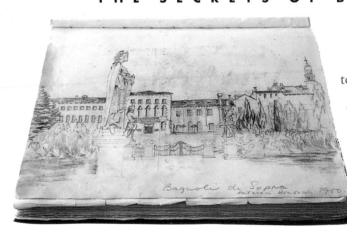

Bagnoli, like Janus, has two faces. The first, turned toward the square, has a Venetian-style façade of sober and elegant proportions whose hermetically sealed doors and windows seem to forbid all contact with the exterior. Watched over by the clock tower of a neighboring church, the house shows a haughty reserve that recalls a far-off past, when the property was in the hands of monks. But one should not trust appearances, especially in Italy, where a stern face often masks hidden beauties. We must thus find the secret of Bagnoli, knocking mightily on the heavy door—the bronze knocker reverberating—until it finally cracks open. It is then that we glimpse the other face of Bagnoli, an enchanted realm open to the sky.

Bagnoli is an enchanted dwelling that opens onto immense vineyards beyond the gardens.

32

*Scorching heat beats down
on the garden, but in the
salon, silent at this hour, all
remains cool and peaceful.
Above a table of carved wood
where the guest books rest
hangs a chandelier of
Venetian glass. The floor is
"seminato," a mixture of
marble fragments and marble
paste; the fireplace, Verona
marble.* OVERLEAF *The
bicolored checkerboard
of the vestibule floor.*

The story of Bagnoli began centuries ago. Duke Almerico of the
Lombards brought this property into the bosom of the Catholic
Church by giving it to the bishop of Padua in 954. In 1656
Bagnoli returned to secular hands when Pope Alexander VII sold
the land to the Widmann counts. It was they who, in the eighteenth
century, were to enlarge the cellars that exist today. In 1917, Rom-
ualdo, the grandfather of Lorenzo, the current proprietor, bought
Bagnoli from the princes of Aremberg. It was a turning point in the
history of the property for, while following its original vocation of
growing wine, it became a family house.

Lorenzo and his brothers and sisters, along with their father and
their mother, Rosalinda, come often to Bagnoli. They come in the
spring because it is so mild, in summer as a matter of course, in

34

autumn to hunt hare and pheasant. The villa is large and always full of company. Rosalinda welcomes with kindness cousins from France and Italy and numerous family friends. Lorenzo drives the tractor and works in the cellars.

In the silence of the grand salon all remains cool and peaceful. Someone, half sunk into a vast white sofa, leafs through the guest books with a lazy finger. Memories flood out with the turning of the pages. Sometimes one lingers over a little remark.

"To my grandparents at Easter. These vacations at Bagnoli are truly marvelous. This garden full of dandelions, these happy bluebells, all that and the animals make this land a paradise." (Carli, April 14, 1971.)

This family paradise is Bagnoli's true secret.

OPPOSITE *The great gallery, decorated by Venetian school paintings.* ABOVE *A bedroom, with its furniture of wrought iron and gilt wood.* OVERLEAF *Behind curtains of leaves, statues are the silent actors of the commedia dell'arte.*

BENEVOLENT SHADOWS

ABOVE *The façade on the garden side, the central part of which dates to the eighteenth century.* OPPOSITE *Dominique watches the children gather blackberries.*

Le Quesnoy appears at the bend of the drive, a big house rising on this July afternoon from a sun-drenched esplanade. In the silence of the heat, the house dozes, folded up behind its shutters. Only a bicycle, thrown down before the threshold, shows the children the presence of their little friends. No sooner has the car stopped than the door opens. Diane-Rose and Stanislas—on the lookout for the arrival of Félicité, Victor, and Alexandre—rush forth in a chorus of happy cries and off they go to the swings.

I can make out in the windows the silhouettes of Hubert and Dominique. I barely enter the cool vestibule with its checkerboard floor when I sense that here the spirit of the place has remained very much the same.

42

PRECEDING PAGES *The salon was remade by Hubert's grandmother with elements of paneling she painted herself.* ABOVE AND OPPOSITE *The boys peer into the salon windows, while the girls read on the Napoleon III family furniture.*

A long time ago, Le Quesnoy was the modest outbuilding of a huge fortified citadel, which, like so many others, did not survive the Revolution. Hubert's ancestors returned to Normandy during the Restoration and enlarged the house of their major domo, which was still standing. Several comfortable marriages later, the family moved to a smart new château at the top of the hill which fully united the architectural inspiration of the nineteenth century with the beginnings of modern comfort. After she was widowed, Hubert's great-grandmother gave her son free rein at the château and came back to Le Quesnoy to settle for good.

The Second World War left Le Quesnoy in a pitiful state. It was necessary to rebuild and restore to make the house live once again. Luckily, the family has an artistic disposition. Hubert's grandmother,

with her husband and sister, performed wonders. They remade, piecemeal, the *boiseries* of the salon with fragments of eighteenth-century armoires, decorated the walls, and hung portraits, flower paintings, and plates.

Hubert's grandmother left Paris at the end of the season to settle at Le Quesnoy from the twenty-fifth of June to the end of October. Hubert and his brothers and sisters returned each year in August to the landscapes, walks, games—all those habits that give summers in family houses their inimitable flavor. They hunted for mushrooms in the Sebastopol woods and chased rabbits among the ferns. They spent long days at the beach, returning to Le Quesnoy exhausted, piled into an old Deux-Chevaux with their pails and shovels and their kites rolled into towels stiff with salt.

OPPOSITE *On the landing of the second floor, a painting by an aunt of Hubert's shows a very nineteenth-century idealized vision of the former vegetable garden.* ABOVE LEFT *In the princess's bedroom, nothing has changed.* ABOVE *A young man's bedroom with its amusing little desk.*

OPPOSITE *As is often the case, the hallway serves as gallery for the artists in the family— here, the canvases of Hubert's grandfather.* LEFT AND ABOVE *The whole house, including the children's rooms, attests to the artistic abilities of the princess, Hubert's grandmother.*

*Country houses are full
of bicycles. Stanislas,
Alexandre, and Victor
leave for a ride.*

Today children head off, armed with baskets, for the blackberry bushes. Tonight for dessert Dominique will place a large dish of blackberries with crème fraîche on the table.

A little later, the girls are in their beds, whispering secrets. The boys, in their room, light bug repellents on the windowsills. In the salon, the parents rest easy. The night slowly envelops them. One senses the presence of benevolent shadows, certainly stirred up by Hubert, who recalls how his brothers and sisters and he always discovered the hiding place for "the Prince's chocolate," the prince being their grandfather, a Russian prince, his head ever covered with a red *chèche* with a black pom-pom. "Grandfather, the essence of indulgence, always looked astonished. 'I just don't understand. When you are here my chocolate disappears so quickly.'"

THE NEW HOMESTEAD

Paula, her daughter, and friends in the gardens of Beaulieu, where each generation has left its own personal mark.

Things being given their due, Beaulieu would have a place in a great saga for its beauty, its presence, its romantic aura. The first chapter of the book would be dominated by the imposing silhouette of its founder, Georges de la Tour, a gentleman of the Périgord who left all that he had known and cherished from his youngest years, to find his fortune far from home. A mystery remains unsolved today: what led Georges to the Napa Valley, a then almost unexplored region at the end of the world? One can imagine his wonder before this limitless landscape where the earth seemed to touch the sky. He bought a piece of land. Georges de la Tour would be both one of the first people to settle in the Napa Valley and one of the first to plant grapevines there.

54

In the 1870s he met the woman who would become his wife, Fernande. A first house was built and three children were born. Life at Beaulieu passed peacefully. Over the years, Fernande de la Tour created magnificent gardens whose Italian inspiration softened the balance of the French spirit. Beaulieu began to produce magnificent wines that would become famous.

One night, just like so many others in the candlelit house, misfortune struck. A fire broke out. Roaring and untameable, the flames devoured everything in their path. By the grace of God, all the residents were safe and sound. Georges de la Tour and his family moved to the foreman's house, which they hastened to enlarge. They would never leave it, starting a new chapter and building the foundations of Beaulieu as we find the house today.

Beaulieu evokes a paradise regained. Long, completely white, underlined by touches of that green always known as Beaulieu green, the house stretches out along the lawn, lengthened by a veranda.

The silent heat of the afternoon is troubled only by the delicate dripping of fountains. The tennis court, deserted at this hour, is hidden behind a rampart of roses. Several steps from the court, also slightly set back, a vegetable garden worthy of a large family stretches out, where Paula, as a child, used to hunt for wild strawberries. On the other side of the river, an *allee* of plane trees, whose branches twist around solid frames, forms a shady vault. Here is a curiosity, due to Paula's grandmother and her Hungarian gardener. Near the entry, where two strong pilasters mark the threshold, is the "friendship garden," where the plants that guests brought to lunches or dinners are tended, witness to the importance placed on that virtue here.

Four generations were once united in the house. As the family gradually grew, bedrooms were added one to another. They all connected. As usual in old houses, they were named by color: "You

ABOVE *Beaulieu is a large and welcoming house where little cousins meet again each summer.*
OPPOSITE *On the white veranda, rows of painted wicker chairs await the many friends of the house.*

ABOVE AND OPPOSITE
*Beaulieu, where four
generations have sometimes
dwelt under the same roof,
grew with the family.*
OVERLEAF *Not very far
from the entrance to Beaulieu,
this delightful cottage is a
perfect introduction to the
main house.*

take the pink bedroom. The blue bedroom is for you." The children
slept there two by two in eighteenth-century-style painted wooden
beds. The furniture could have belonged to a country house. If it
were not for the vast American landscape, one could believe that one
was in France. His extraordinary success in the New World did not
make Georges or his children forget the southwest of France. They
passed four or five months each year on the continent. It is not
surprising that his daughter married a Frenchman.

The inhabitants of Beaulieu are like that, open to the outside
world, passionate, proud of their origins, faithful to their new
homeland. The impalpable timelessness that reigns at Beaulieu is the
result of the osmosis Georges sought between two cultures, one
young, the other very old, cohabiting harmoniously.

SUMMERS IN ITALY

A family portrait in the house that Olivier and Anne have been restoring for ten years.

I was nine . . . twelve . . . fourteen years old. I spent several weeks each summer in the same place in the country. I knew it by heart! My parents, and adults in general—things have greatly changed since then—hardly worried about keeping us busy and even less about keeping us amused.

In the morning, especially when the weather was good, there was always something to do: go on errands, go to Sunday mass, go horseback riding before it became too hot and the horseflies invaded. Lunchtime came very, very quickly. But the afternoon was another story. How long they seemed to me sometimes. "Get out," we were told. "Get some fresh air," "walk," no matter what, but we were to stay outside until snacktime. Complying, we only dreamed of one thing: to slip quietly into the warm atmosphere of the kitchen, where a wood stove purred day and night, to watch television. At that time, television was a novelty. It had the taste of forbidden fruit, and we used all our wiles to achieve our ends!

Being thus left to our own devices might have inspired us to great pranks. But, apart from several notable moments—such as the day

when the Vespa carrier that we were forbidden to use plunged into the river with Alain behind the handlebars and a whole group of adolescents in the rear—we were rather well behaved. In fact, we gave free rein to our imaginations. From one summer to the next, we outdid ourselves in inventing great games that took over the garden and

entire afternoons. These games, depending upon the number of participants, sometimes degenerated into true clan wars that could last for entire weeks. Battles drawn up at the back of the vegetable garden, commando operations, warlike songs, spies, secret meetings of chiefs and their troops having retreated to the woodshed, the billiard room, or the landing of the top floor—we threw ourselves into the game. Traditionally, the English crossed swords with the French, the Cowboys with the Indians. There was always something

67

PRECEDING PAGES
Harmonious sobriety in the salon, decorated with frescoes painted by Giuseppe Mattia Borgnis around 1720.
OPPOSITE AND ABOVE *In family houses one finds furniture one will see nowhere else, long empty corridors, and space for pianos.*

TOP AND RIGHT *Everyone has a role to play: while Mado prepares lunch, it is Clémence's turn to set the table.* ABOVE *A relic from another life, when the house was a hotel.*

glorious about being part of the band of Indians, even if the Indians were roundly beaten.

Much of the fun has to do with the number of children taking part in games, and certain families are decidedly more favored. Olivier, Jean-Louis, and their already numerous brothers and sisters returned each August to more than fifty cousins—ideal for the making of large Indian tribes. This concentration is explained by the attachment that the branches of their family have always felt for the small Lombard village that is their place of origin.

"You have to know that in the north of Italy, as in Scotland, the men left to find their fortune elsewhere," explains Olivier, the depositary of all the anecdotes of the family saga, thanks to long conversations he undertook from year to year with his old aunts. "Our ancestors arrived in France in 1515, leaving their wives at home, of course. At the beginning of the seventeenth century, the Lombard community, having foiled a plot against Louis XIII, benefited from the protection of the regent, Marie de Médicis. This protection, which was renewed with each reign, permitted the family to carry on its trade without paying taxes. Faithful to their roots, the men returned home regularly from the other side of the Alps. Then they left in couples, always returning to finish their days in their own country. Until 1850, all the men of the family married women from the valley. Inevitably richer than the others, the 'expatriates' were kind of benefactors to the village. They all owned homes. Certain ones still belong to our seventh-generation cousins. Cousins who we only see here."

Several steps from the church, the family property where Olivier, Jean-Louis, and their cousin Françoise passed the summer is made up of several houses in a row. One of them, the largest, was left by the grandfather to three of his children. It was thus divided into three

ABOVE *Play of light and shadows in the central staircase.* OPPOSITE *Olivier finds Constance immersed in a comic book on a second-floor landing big enough to house a small library.*

*Jean-Louis finds the garden
of his childhood once again.*

parts, with three different staircases. This pattern continued outside, with three gardens. "During moments of family tension," recall the cousins, "we children were sent each to our own garden to play without going beyond the boundaries, while our parents watched each other from afar over the hedges."

Each age has its own games and its memories. When there are so many children returning each summer over so many years, these times spent together create a complicity which time can never completely erase.

There were often so many in residence that three meals at a time had to be planned. The little ones went first, then the middle ones, and finally the eldest. The adults organized picnics, races, costume parties, tennis tournaments. They had their coffee on the terrace, making plans for the afternoon, while below the children snuck about the vegetable garden, stealing strawberries. The cousins fished for tadpoles in the cistern, returning home to be scolded, dripping wet from head to toe.

The statue of the Sacred Heart in the garden became a stronghold to defend with one's life. Some mounted guard, the others attacked. The prisoners, tied to trees, were attacked by ants!

"Then came the time of great hikes. We left for two days with our sleeping bags. We set off around seven o'clock in the evening and hiked all night in order to see the rising sun on the Mont Rose chain. After each trip, we came back with new stories, new memories. Very quickly I understood that to have a family house was a great privilege," explains Olivier. "I wanted the same thing for my children."

Over the course of inheritances, a gift of property to the eldest with the obligation to welcome his brothers and sisters, aunts, and uncles has allowed the ties to the village to be maintained. Olivier

ABOVE *From the second floor of the house where Olivier's grandparents once lived, one looks down onto the terrace where everyone gathers for coffee in the summer.*
OPPOSITE *A Virgin and Child watch over the family.*

74

and his family came as guests until the day they decided to find a place of their own. But not just anywhere! "I looked for a place that had belonged to our family in the past. One day I learned that a hotel-restaurant located just behind the church was closing down. I went to one of my aunts to convince her to let me take over this house and return it to its original purpose as a family house. Luckily, I succeeded, for I, too, like my family before me, need to come here to replenish myself." Ten years and mountains of work later, the house has found a new life, its daily routine punctuated by the chimes of the church bells.

It is morning, one of those delicate mornings when the light is so transparent that one can make out the slightest fold of the landscape in the distance. On the terrace, the breakfast table is set. Emilie,

OPPOSITE AND ABOVE *In the little wood-paneled salon and the adjoining room with its painted ceiling, a whole life peopled with a thousand memories.*

ABOVE AND RIGHT

Nineteenth-century furniture, engravings, a mirror in a gilt-wood frame—all reflect the timeless atmosphere of a bedroom. OPPOSITE *In Italy, painters went from house to house, decorating the walls with naïve frescoes.*

having finished her last piece of bread, sits down at the piano. The notes of music float outside where we are reading the news, having a last coffee behind a wall of newspapers opened wide. Clémence, who has already changed two times, appears in the doorway, with starlet glasses perched on her nose. Their brother Charles is not there yet but he will soon join us.

Yes, life has begun again in the harmony of the large, light rooms, and the present, very gently, prepares for the future.

C O M B E R M E R E   A B B E Y

ABOVE *A pure example of neo-Gothic style.*
OPPOSITE *In the hall, the great-grandmother of Sarah and her daughter, Frederica, rub elbows with impressive trophies.*

Our story begins quite a long time ago, in 1131, with the installation of a handful of monks led by Hugues de Malblanc somewhere in Cheshire. Here in the heart of this fertile, green, and gently rolling countryside, Cistercians, known for their sense of beauty, found the solitude and harmony they were seeking.

The main abbey was built to be reflected with the sky on the mirrored surface of a large body of water. In the cruel disorder of the Reformation, the monks disappeared and their monastery was razed, with the exception of the residence of the father abbot. A companion of Henry VIII, Sir George Cotton, enlarged this building and made it worthy of himself. Over the course of centuries one transformation followed another. The most spectacular took place in

80

the beginning of the nineteenth century, when the first Viscount
Combermere adorned the old manor with the elegant stone
lacework of the then-fashionable Gothic style and constructed vast
outbuildings, an enclosed garden, and splendid stables.

The third Viscount lost his fortune, and the property underwent
an eclipse. The fourth Viscount took advantage of the calm that
followed the First World War and sold the property. A new chapter
began for Combermere Abbey with its entry in 1919 into the family
of Sarah, the current proprietor.

The Combermere Abbey of Sarah's youth was always an
animated house. It was in the surrounding hills that she learned to
ride. It was on its peaceful lake that she launched her boat and lost
herself in the contemplation of the clouds. The old greenhouses,

OPPOSITE *The curves of a
nineteenth-century Italian
gilt-wood console stand out
against a ground of dark
paneling.* ABOVE *The dining
room contains English and
Dutch furniture of the
eighteenth century. The
immense oak table dates
from the end of the
seventeenth century.*

On a sofa in the library,
covered in the family tartan,
two young accomplices,
Peregrine and his cousin
Benjamin.

half-abandoned, overflowed with peaches and figs that Sarah and her two sisters gathered. "There was so much space that one had an impression of complete freedom," she remembers. "The house is so big that there are rooms on the upper floors where no one had entered for ages and that never changed."

Like all young people, Sarah felt the call of the outside world. She tackled New York, remaining for eighteen years. Independent, without special ties, a public relations officer for a large company, she lost the habit of living in England. But when Sarah realized she could, if she wished, inherit Combermere, with its miles of roofs, its hundreds of acres, she accepted the challenge. Her installation at Combermere took place in 1992.

On Midsummer's Day Sarah gathered around her two hundred of

her friends, costumed as lords and ladies of the sixteenth century. The guests, rustling in their silks, brocades, feathers, and jewels, descended from their barges before the house lit by torches. Later, the island would be ablaze with fireworks, while in the center, the bonfire of a straw castle would shoot forth a shower of sparks into the night. Parties are lovely because they are ephemeral, and life is good for it always has surprises in store. It had one for Sarah. The surprise was Peter, who had always lived a few miles from Combermere, but whom she had never met before then.

Destiny had undoubtedly decided this. It was necessary for her to follow the road to Combermere to find Peter awaiting her. Today there are three of them to assure the future of their house. Peregrine, when he grows up, will take up the torch.

OPPOSITE *The salon is representative of the beginnings of neo-Gothic architecture.* ABOVE *The bed, designed by Peter, was given to his wife as a wedding gift.* OVERLEAF *From the back of the house, the view at Combermere opens onto parkland filled with ancient oaks and what was described in 1892 as "the finest sheet of water in any park in England."*

A WEDDING AT RARAY

We all feel a special tenderness for the places that have marked our youth. As for me, I have lodged in my heart a place I always think of with the same emotion and which I see exactly as it was during the time when we were all united there in a joyous carelessness. If I doubted the existence of happiness for an instant, I would need only to evoke Raray to have the proof that it exists against wind and tides.

I remember everything as if it were yesterday. The aromas that snuck out of the kitchen where Sophie fluttered about like an orchestra conductor before her stoves, sautéing tons of potatoes cut into thin rounds in immense black pans. I remember the sound of the ringing of the telephone placed on a little table at the top of the stairs. I even remember that in that region there were still operators. One raised the handpiece, dialed a number, then, to the anonymous voice that answered, politely asked for "fourteen in Barbery" or "nineteen in Senlis." Yet, it wasn't very long ago.

Certain sounds come back with the seasons. Every August the dull rumbling of the harvesters made the night vibrate. Others became so familiar—here I think of the wild cavalcades of the dormice in the attic above our bedrooms—that one no longer paid attention.

The colors, too, I have not forgotten. The salon was furnished in dark wood; the sofa Yvonne, countess and lady of the house, usually occupied, accompanied by a piece of work or a book, always serene and attentive, was covered in a very soft green velvet. There were also armchairs in which Miss Downie, the old nanny of Marino,

A flower in the buttonhole of Jean-Marc and his future son-in-law, Amaury; a cloud of tulle for Tatiana. . . . The final preparations for a lovely wedding.

90

dozed in turn. The armchairs, undoubtedly because of the "old rose" fabric that covered them, had about them something a bit "Parisian," therefore vaguely out of the ordinary. But above all, facing the fireplace, was a huge studded leather armchair, well worn, that belonged to a marvelous man, a true gentleman, Count Antoine. The whole room revolved around him.

Count Antoine was tall, a bit portly. Of an absolute elegance in his subtle tweeds, he stood very straight and wore his bow tie with an authority like no one else. He was goodness, and, to us, indulgence itself. He had a singular sense of humor and a clear and generous view of life. After lunch, everyone gathered around him for coffee. We laughed and chattered like magpies for hours. Then, dressed in our loden with Tyrolian caps, we left to walk in the

woods, toward the Porte Rouge where reigned in majesty the Lady
with the Unicorn.

At Raray, one was always welcomed with open arms. For
Yvonne, to entertain one more person at the last moment was of no
importance. We squeezed in a bit around the table and added one
more place setting. That was all. There was always food enough for
another. She sometimes gave the impression that the treasure of
kindness and tenderness that she had within her could include the
entire world and not drain her. Around the family was a close circle
of friends, a kind of adopted family of the heart—those who came all
the time, like me, Robert, Dominique, François, Florence, Alain,
Bertrand, and all the others.

Each child in the family had his group of friends. Jean-Marc had

his friends, of which I was one. We were sandwiched between those of Yves and Thérèse, the eldest, and those of Marino, the youngest, who seemed to us then really very young. The older ones viewed us in the same way. Yves, who had just become engaged, gave us an absent look, while the suitors of Thérèse seemed the height of sophistication to us: Several of them had their driver's licenses and their independence made us burn with envy. Imagine! But Jean-Marc found a not very rapid but ingenious solution to link the several-mile distance between the house of my aunt and Raray. I will always remember his arrival, perched on an enormous tractor that pulled behind it a trailer full of straw. We all piled on—direction Raray—and made our way under the sun, very slowly and by way of little country roads.

The comings and goings by tractor only lasted for a while. But they marked a kind of transition, for after that summer we quickly caught up with Thérèse and her friends. We noticed with great satisfaction that we had the same pursuits as they; soon we had the same driver's licenses.

We came together, for there was no reason to stay apart. What did we do? Well, we did what one always does in the country. From the depths of our deck chairs, we remade the world peacefully, without hurrying. This was a blessed period, with no storms other than those of the first beatings of our hearts. What was important for us was to be together.

Together, as we are today when we find ourselves again around Tatiana, the oldest daughter of Jean-Marc, who is to marry Amaury. Together, because life has given us this lovely location for reuniting. Together, precisely because friendship does not recognize passing time. Together, because Raray will remain for us, no matter what happens, a place apart.

ABOVE AND OPPOSITE
Weddings, communions, birthdays . . . these simple and happy events mark the life of family houses over the years.

94

THE CHATEAU OF LA BAUME

The château of La Baume rises up on a fanned-out plateau, rooted in the swells of the meadows like a stone ship. The high walls of granite conceal a self-enclosed world that awakens each spring when the fields bedeck themselves with gentian and heather and that retreats with the arrival of the first frost. This self-sufficient universe is protected by its isolation in the midst of a proud and savage countryside.

La Baume is the place where Geneviève, her sisters, and brother grew up, the land of their childhood. The immense corridors monitored by their ancestors from their frames, the silent salons, the vast bedrooms lorded over by baldachin beds in dark woods, the mysterious locked rooms, deep armoires piled up with linens and

ABOVE *Two friends, Privat and Astorg, in the central courtyard.* OPPOSITE *A puzzle of tiles and dormers.*

96

*Philippine's wedding dress
has been put away from
prying eyes in the King's
Bedroom with its
Louis XIII paneling.*

memories, never held any secrets for them. At the very bottom of the house, far from the dining room, the sonorous kitchen shelters regiments of pots whose copper shines against the walls. Way up high under the roof, one discovers very old attics where marvelous treasures have accumulated over the centuries under a coat of dust. There are shadowy areas, nooks and crannies, trapdoors, doors that grate, floors that creak, noises that disturb the calm of the night. But nothing frightens children when they know a house by heart, even if they admit preferring to "sleep with others." At La Baume, it was at nightfall—an especially favorable time for the shivers—that one told the most beautiful and most terrifying stories. Like that of the Seigneur César de Grolée, called "the Great Caesar," who was always accompanied by two formidable Great Danes, and so terrified the region in the seventeenth century that even today one threatens impossible children with being carried off by this dark and violent figure.

Each vacation—All Saints' Day, Easter, and the summer months—gave Geneviève the chance to regain La Baume. Eight hours of travel, numerous rest stops, always a sick child. Sometimes a breakdown slowed the movement even more. One had to "earn" La Baume. But, when the car at last slowly took the turn onto the dirt road that led to the château, its exhausted cargo miraculously found itself resuscitated!

Free, let loose in nature, the six children, to which were always added several of their thirty cousins, again found the simple pleasures of their age. "We each had a cow," remembers Geneviève, "and we would run to talk with them. They had names that were traditionally those of the Countesses of La Baume. At five o'clock on the dot, all the children disappeared—it was time for milking."

The call to order came several times a day when the heavy clock near the front door rang mealtime. At the first striking, one washed

ABOVE *A moment of contemplation in the attic for Michel.*
OPPOSITE *The walls of the great vaulted staircase are entirely decorated with grisaille paintings.*

100

ABOVE *The charm of an old armoire piled up with linens.* TOP *The cake cupboard, which resembles a tabernacle, is only opened at snack time.* CENTER AND RIGHT *The formal dining room with its shelves of glass jars and its cabinets of old faïence. The coffered ceiling and walls are decorated with a collection of plates.*

one's hands. At the second, one sat down to eat. Lunch and dinner were unbending gatherings when the children had the right to be present but not to be noticed: "the best way to remind the wild shoots that we were of good manners." After dinner, the bell rang again. The party then moved to the chapel, where prayers lasted half an hour. Guests were not exempt. The first time they were thunderstruck, because it seemed they had stepped into a bygone world. Yet uncontrollable laughter was common. Those who laughed too noticeably were sent away—the height of good fortune!

Easter and Holy Week, however—punctuated by masses and pilgrimages—were taken very seriously by the family. "We walked for miles, and we had to have our prayers at our fingertips. For the slightest hesitation we were denied a meal."

The family dining room and its portrait gallery of ancestors, witness to renowned disputes and reconciliations.

103

BELOW *This armor could have been that of the Great Caesar!* RIGHT *At La Baume, children become "big" when they have crossed the hallway in shivers all alone at night.* OPPOSITE *In the salon, Privat plays dominoes under the watchful eye of the Sun King.*

ABOVE *Two great attractions of the summer: fishing for crayfish and picnicking by the pond in the old family Jeep.* OPPOSITE, TOP *The château of La Baume.* OPPOSITE, BOTTOM *Henri, Privat, Maguelonne, and May with their picnic baskets.*

ABOVE *"Crayfish fishing" in the Pompeian bedroom.* ABOVE, RIGHT *The sun of La Baume.* OPPOSITE *May dreaming in the Pompeian bedroom where Geneviève's great-grandfather had all his favorite activities painted in the form of allegories in 1880. Above the bed the scene evokes his passion for a new invention: the automobile.*

During these very harsh beginnings of spring, the children gathered before bedtime around a stove that provided heat. They then galloped through chilly corridors to see who could reach his bed first. This life was sometimes difficult, without complacency, without useless luxury, yet happy and free, marked by unforgettable moments.

With time, the ties that bound Geneviève to La Baume, far from loosening, were reinforced. She could never have married a man who did not "understand" La Baume. But with Michel, she had nothing to fear. Geneviève's territory soon became his own. In turn, they have taught their children the meaning of territory, a word that rings with the echo of olden times. A word of memory that evokes belonging. A word that is embodied in the château of La Baume, rooted in the swells of the meadows like a stone ship.

108

THE MANOR OF KERDAOUALAS

ABOVE *Kerdaoualas stands proudly on top of a hill.*
BELOW AND OPPOSITE *Victoire and Alexandra take their daily walk.*

Gray as the waves on a February afternoon, mauve as a carpet of heather, bright as a bouquet of gorse, Brittany, in the far west of France, is a wild territory nourished by its isolation. Before it, nothing except the immensity of the sea, the air laden with salt. It is an austere landscape, drawn in ink. But when the sun appears and wipes away the shadows of the storm, one suddenly feels the earth, bathed in light, shiver in golden astonishment.

A land of fairies, a land of saints, Brittany lives in the whisper of its legends and mysteries. Strange Brittany, whose sons, rocked by the magical rhythm of bombardon and bagpipes, sailors or farmers, are kings; her daughters, in their embroidered dress and coiffed with their light crown of lace, are queens. . . . Here the past and present

110

are intimately linked, like life and death. And where the Bretons believe in a parallel universe peopled by mocking spirits and often lost souls.

Catherine, newly married, was surprised to see on one of her first trips to the peninsula, that the old family cook—sixty years in the house—never swept her kitchen in the evening, so great was her fear of driving away the spirits of the dead who always search the comfort of a warm and welcoming place at night.

In Brittany the ties that bind the farmers to their land, the sailors to their boats, are impossible to unravel, as are those that link families within themselves. In Brittany, one is always somehow someone's cousin. All the neighbors in the countryside around Joseph and Catherine share a link of kinship with them. This develops a strong

The decor of the manor, warm and a bit austere at the same time, is well suited to Brittany.

113

RIGHT AND BELOW *Catherine chose a theme for each bedroom; here, the marine room.* OPPOSITE *The games room, with its massive carved-wood billiard table, is the refuge of rainy days.*

feeling of belonging, which accompanies Bretons from their first to their last breath.

To marry a Breton is, in fact, to marry Brittany. For Catherine, this meant penetrating a true clan taken root there for five hundred years. A manor, the traditional dwelling of a Breton gentleman,

114

situated between a château and a small countryseat, was therefore one of her wedding presents. It was Kerdaoualas, situated on a hill near Brest and whose silhouette dominated both the sea and the countryside.

Kerdaoualas, "the house of the two murders," was named because

of a bloody scuffle between two monks after a game of cards. This was in the thirteenth century, when there was only a large defensive tower to which the peasants came to protect themselves from attacks from the sea. To this tower was added the body of the main building in 1600, then a large salon in the 1700s—it was in the spirit of the times—and finally, a kind of excrescence, which, even if it seems today to be the most authentic part of the house, only dates to the very late nineteenth century.

Kerdaoualas entered into the family about a century ago, when Joseph's great-grandfather, the admiral, bought it, his brother having taken over the manor in Quimperlé. Two generations later, it was the place where Joseph spent his childhood. It was there that he passed his adolescence and the war. It is a place he knows by heart and for which he feels a visceral attachment. Alas, a first cousin inherited it. But curiously, and one must undoubtedly say happily, the cousin's wife, in spite of eight children, found the manor too large and refused to move in. By one of those strokes of luck that enrich life, Joseph owned a house in the center of Brittany. It suited the cousin. The exchange was made. To find himself at twenty-two years old at the head of an immense house, to be totally redone, did not daunt him. He had finally come back to port.

After her marriage, Catherine found the manor in a sad state. It had been closed for ten years, humidity seeped out everywhere, the roof was full of leaks, rain entered by the second floor, the rooms were empty of furniture. There was a single bathroom. To bring Kerdaoualas out of its lethargy would take patience and tenacity, two typically Breton qualities. For years, Catherine and Joseph transformed themselves into electricians, upholsterers. Catherine spent years perched on a ladder, hanging fabric on the walls of thirty rooms. They scoured the neighborhood's second-hand shops, for they needed furniture to give the manor its proud look of past days!

Two boys were born, Thomas and Adrien. Like their father, they will bring an unconditional love to Kerdaoualas.

Having become Breton in spirit, Catherine opened Kerdaoualas to the whole family. Nephews and nieces, cousins are welcomed with joy. They feel at home here and that is what Catherine intends.

Kerdaoualas likes to be inhabited. Otherwise—Catherine has noticed it—the manor turns in on itself and becomes humid again, as if suffering from melancholy. One must never lose sight of the fact that a house is a living thing, and to bring a family house back to life is never an insignificant procedure. For Joseph, the manor symbolizes permanence across time, for Catherine a patrimony of love.

PRECEDING PAGES *The grand salon, its furniture still covered with winter slipcovers.* OPPOSITE *Precious porcelains on an exceptional seventeenth-century gilt-wood console table with a hunting motif.* ABOVE *In the spring, the salon wakes up bit by bit.*

119

ABOVE AND RIGHT *In the blue bedroom, which has a dressing room as in the past, Catherine had the good idea of regrouping several family photographs and miniatures in large frames.* OPPOSITE *A lovely way of keeping the past present: coats of arms, portraits of ancestors, menus from parties are hung along ribbons.*

ABOVE *Victoire and Alexandra on vacation.* RIGHT *Kerdaoualas "the house of the two murders," was named because of a bloody scuffle between two monks in the thirteenth century after a game of cards. Between the seventeenth and the nineteenth centuries the manor grew, each generation leaving its mark.*

A New Generation

Setting Down Roots

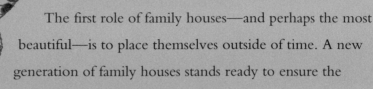

The first role of family houses—and perhaps the most beautiful—is to place themselves outside of time. A new generation of family houses stands ready to ensure the succession without shedding contemporary imagery.

The desire to set down roots somewhere is, above all, the beginning of an interior adventure shared by several people—one that has nothing to do with feeling out of one's element. In fact, when the moment comes, one goes instinctively toward a familiar region or perhaps a place where one could *imagine* having spent one's own childhood.

These new family houses—new because one settles there as a first generation—are often extremely old. The play of influences is subtle. They must be compatible with the memories one carries within, but also ready to welcome others.

The themes interpreted there will not be new. Think, instead, rejuvenation, recaptured with different variations. We all have the memory of associations of color and materials, of an accumulation of objects, of those thousand-and-one details that express a family's taste. The taste that belongs to it alone. We remember dark wooden furniture against light walls. We still breathe in, many years later, the perfume of armfuls of lilacs that blends with that of beeswax.

This new generation will quickly find the regular and unchangeable rhythm of family houses—the rhythm that reassures, that upholds and gives to things their true proportions. For here we are not speaking of breaks but of continuity.

THE PAST REGAINED

ABOVE AND OPPOSITE

The present house, which dates from the sixties, was enlarged by David and Kim. OVERLEAF *The proud silhouette of the Castle of Appin, seat of the Stewart of Appin's clan, dominates the loch.*

Wisps of fog stretch out over the loch whose flat surface gives slate-colored reflections. On the opposite bank, the powerful swelling of the hills rises toward the black sky like the breaths of a giant.

Several yards from the house, David, in his moss-colored tweeds, strides across the meadow, making a path in the high grass. The way he sometimes stops, looking about him, shows that he is truly the master of this estate at the end of the world, that this magnificent and savage land where nothing save lichen grows is truly his. That its blood, the blood of this earth, courses in his veins.

The Highlands, with landscapes imbued with a bewitching beauty, is a land of extremes. A land of storms, swept by wind and rain, it nourishes men of irreducible bravery. A romantic and violent

land, it carries within it the echo of terrible battles. A land so poor that its sons, from all time, have left to seek their fortunes elsewhere. But yes, they come back.

The story of David's family is inscribed in that of the Highlands. His ancestors trod the soil where he walks today and their eyes surveyed the same unchangeable landscape. Since the fourteenth century, David and his own have been at home here.

"In 1513," he recounts, "after the battle of Flodden Field against the English—a disaster for our troops, who suffered dreadful losses there—my ancestor did something uncharacteristically Scottish. His six sons returned alive and covered in glory from this slaughter, so he decided to abandon inheritance by primogeniture. Instead, he divided his land among them, reserving only a larger parcel for the eldest. I am

a descendant of the fourth son to whom this land of Fasnacloich had come."

Until the end of the seventeenth century, in this universe of solitudes, the family preferred to live in a manor set back on the heights. Then they came down to the edge of the lake. The first house built on the present site was in no way a castle, for the Highland earth proved not very generous. Until the beginning of the twentieth century, the house grew with the rhythm of good fortune and births. But, what often happens in old families occurred. The cousin to whom it belonged was driven to ruin and had to sell it. It thus passed into the hands of a rich industrialist to whom it represented nothing. Its allure, on the whole modest, did it a disservice. It was razed. In its place an enormous crenellated

OPPOSITE *In the vast gallery, furnished with rattan sofas and armchairs, the windows are oriented toward the loch.* ABOVE *The indispensable cloakroom where hunting jackets, raincoats, various hats, and fishing poles accumulate along with the obligatory assortment of boots.* OVERLEAF *To choose a tablecloth using a family tartan is a Scottish custom: here, the Hunting Stewart.*

133

structure was erected. No doubt this better corresponded to the recent fortune of the industrialist.

David, raised about six miles from there, on the other side of the hill, was not unaware of this story. The castle was too large, badly built, with a flat roof poorly adapted to this rainy climate. David watched this Edwardian absurdity deteriorate bit by bit. He was eight years old. Already he had an unyielding determination, and he formed the idea of returning to Fasnacloich.

In the 1960s, one of David's friends acquired what was no more than a vestige of the castle. The wood paneling was removed and the shell dynamited. The white house topped with a gray roof he now lives in dates from this era.

Three times Fasnacloich had eluded David. This only intensified his desire to possess it. It took him more than thirty years to recover the inheritance of the fourth son. Today, Kim, his wife from Chicago, and Emily, William, Alexander, and Duncan, his children, know that at Fasnacloich they are at home since always and for always.

OPPOSITE *A lovely decorative element: tartans cover the sofas and the floors as well.* ABOVE LEFT *In a bedroom, an attractive mixture of flowers, tweeds, and plaids.* ABOVE *Duncan, James, and Elizabeth in the medallion.* OVERLEAF *Highland landscapes are imbued with bewitching beauty.*

137

THE HOUSE ON THE LAKE

TOP AND OPPOSITE *From Pasquaney, one has a view plunging down toward the lake.* ABOVE *Scott, Gigi, and their children, Brooks and Emily.*

"We were getting closer to the house. The landscape became more and more familiar and my heart beat faster and faster. Seated next to my father, I took pleasure in anticipating each new turn in the road. I greeted the trees on the sides of the road as if I were seeing old acquaintances again. I hunted for the entrance to the property. I wanted to be the first to see the house." Like a caged bird who is finally going to regain its freedom, John, a little boy of six, hurled himself from the seat of the barely stopped car to take possession of the place without delay.

That year, the freshly painted house seemed particularly natty to him. The tracery of wood that underlined the roof and the windows, a pretty smooth white, stood out clearly against the creamy yellow of

140

the walls. To see it so welcoming, so well maintained, gave the boy a deep flush of euphoria and he leaned, a bit dangerously, over the railing that surrounded the porch. From there, he had a view plunging down to the lake, to the wooden wharf, and to the raft that gently floated several yards from the shore.

Certain years canoes appeared. Gliding through the water, they left a silent wake behind them. For John, this was a good omen.

The house, built on the steep slopes of Newfound Lake, seemed suspended in the midst of trees that gave the many children of the family the impression of living in an enormous and comfortable tree house. A rustic stair, tumbling down the slope of full-grown pines, led directly to the boathouse.

John, after taking his fill of the immense landscape and having reassured himself that there, on the other side of the lake, the dense line of black trees still leaned with the same opacity against the bluish horizon, went inside. Here, too, nothing ever changed. And he liked that. He tried the rocking chairs, slid a light hand over the surface of the venerable dining table, saluted the family photos, and even— once in the kitchen— the old woodstove, still cold, but which, as soon as it was relit, would demand numerous loads of logs. He knew the house by heart.

His parents were married at Pasquaney in the 1920s. They quickly had many children who ran outside during the day and slept under a tent at night. In 1927 they decided that it was time to build a second house. It was thus that Twin Oaks—which was soon to become the wildest of infirmaries, housing during epidemics of measles up to five young patients installed in little camp beds along the chimney of the living room—came to be added to the big house and its annexes— ice house, laundry, garages—forming a kind of small village that was reborn each summer at the dawn of the sunny month of July.

OPPOSITE *John's parents built Pasquaney in the twenties.*
TOP *Almost a tree house.*
ABOVE *Blowing bubbles— the younger generation.*

Today John is eighty and has nine children to whom he has passed his love for Pasquaney and its traditions. Even when their origins have become hazy, they are the charm of a family house. So each morning at precisely nine o'clock all generations gather together in the dining room for a hearty breakfast, and woe unto him who arrives late! Coffee and maple syrup flow generously. John is at the stove.

Earthly nourishment holds an important place in the life of family houses because it is around the table that everyone is reunited three times a day. This ritual allows no exception. Everything stops at the sacred meal hour. Everyone carefully unfolds a white napkin, or a checked one, or a paper one, and casts an eye on the dish placed at the center of the table, then begins to talk, to tell stories, to make

Few things have changed over the years, for Pasquaney is a place full of memories.

144

The kitchen has kept its old woodstove. Next to it, two old hot water heaters and a chair that has seen many babies pass by seem relics of the past.

plans for the next day. The boys are always hungry and take seconds of everything; the girls pick at their food. Then there are those customs linked to the appearance of certain desserts. For example, at John's house blueberry pie puts the little ones in a trance and sets off true fits of happiness from anticipation, for the first one to make a stain is picked up and carried to be thrown pitilessly and fully clothed into the lake.

Thanksgiving—celebrated at Pasquaney a month and a half in advance of the rest of America—is the ceremony that brings down the curtain on the summer. John's family devotes the second weekend of October to it, and there are often more than sixty people. Certain ones bring turkeys, others take the responsibility for mince pies. In the kitchen, people busy themselves around huge pots filled with sweet potato purée and saucepans of peas. Excitement and good humor are widespread.

In the living room and the dining room, which are open to each other, a huge table in the form of a horseshoe has been set up, covered in a collection of table linen. As soon as the preparations are complete, the house becomes calm for a moment, so that everyone can get dressed and those members of the family of Scottish origin can put on their kilts.

After the feast comes the eagerly awaited hour of the performances. The tables are pushed back and chairs are removed to make a place for the actors. Sketches, mimes, poems, pieces of music, all prepared in greatest secrecy, follow one after the other until late in the evening. The children, arranged by size, backs to the fireplace, sing their lungs out. There is always a baby sleeping in a corner whom nothing can arouse. There is also always an amateur photographer whose pictures will be patiently glued, on a rainy day, onto the gray pages of albums and labeled with care.

SHAKER INSPIRATION

Here is a place preserved, where time seems to have stood still.

We are in an extraordinary place—a preserved place so perfectly harmonious that the hand of God seems to have been slowed while giving its gifts a little longer here than elsewhere. It is an old farm, built around 1850, whose silhouette, painted in white, projects from a green bower. One can tell that the site of the simple house, with its adjoining barn, was chosen with the greatest of care by its first occupants. In the kind shadow of immense trees, the farm asserts itself with true sobriety. A little farther, a pond shimmers under the caresses of the breeze. In the center is an island, fully occupied by a century-old oak tree.

Moisha greets us with a smile and explains

148

right away that she has realized a childhood dream. When she was little, she fell in love with those real American houses made of wood like this one. The idea of one day owning one in which to establish a family never left her. She promised herself that she would not betray the spirit of the place, and she kept her promise. Welcoming, sober, and sophisticated, the house resembles her. One senses an extreme attention to detail, which suggests a perfectionist, and a love of objects and paintings, which attests to a very assertive taste, very personal and totally indifferent to the ebb and flow of fashion.

On the ground floor one finds an almost willfully empty space, where the wooden furniture is drawn in large strokes on the surfaces of the walls; windows, all bare, mark off fragments of landscape. There are very few pieces of furniture, but each one counts.

Each spot, as one walks from room to room, evokes a moment of life. One imagines winter meals around the long farmhouse table when it is so cold outside and the adjoining kitchen, in the warmth of its ovens, is in joyful disarray. The living room, crowded around the fireplace, evokes hours of reading and conversation. On the second floor, two small rooms, very simple, one with a desk, indicate the presence of two little boys who have grown up.

Time passes without haste. And then, all of a sudden, autumn arrives and the temperature becomes cool. Above the house, the leaves become deep red cascades. Still Moisha, Bob, Nicholas, and Max gather on the terrace for breakfast, their legs wrapped in blankets. For when one has realized one's dream, one does not rush to relinquish it.

ABOVE AND OPPOSITE *Lit by a thirties hanging lantern, the nineteenth-century farm table in the dining room is surrounded by Thonet chairs.* OVERLEAF *A beautiful marriage of sobriety and color defines this room where Squatter naps.*

153

THE CHATEAU OF VILLERAY

ABOVE AND OPPOSITE

Villeray, a Renaissance château in an English-style park. BELOW *A member of the family, Jim, the labrador.*

"Bonne Maman was incredible. I can still see her. She was nearly six feet tall, had big blue eyes, white hair, and long legs. All winter long she wore a black dress with white dots, in summer, a white dress with black dots. She lived with Bon Papa, who had a cider mill and about a hundred orchards in a village in le Perche, the region where I was born."

Children's lives might be quite monotonous if they were not peopled by astonishing individuals—individuals capable of charming a child's life. With their infallible instincts, they sniff out these beings, gifted by happiness, and attach themselves to them like trusting little puppies. This is why Catherine never tired of vacations with her grandparents, four times a year for sixteen years. It would

156

ABOVE *Here, landings are more than just places of passage.* OPPOSITE, TOP *When it rains, the children move the Chippendale-style chairs and turn the dining table into a Ping-Pong table.* OPPOSITE, BOTTOM *In the salon, eighteenth-century paneling and velvet-covered armchairs create a comfortable atmosphere.*

seem these vacations were heavily laden with good memories, for here she is, back at Villeray.

But let's go back. It is summer. Bon Papa goes to fetch his granddaughter at Prés-en-Paille. They have lunch together, without hurrying, before setting forth to the arms of Bonne Maman. She waits for them at their brick house, the summer house, located at the end of the village.

In the summer, the little girl, bursting with energy, was sometimes entrusted to Madeleine. Madeleine, who has never developed a wrinkle and still lives in Villeray! Certain afternoons, buzzing with sunlight, found them arm in arm, heading for the washhouse. There, kneeling on the cool stone floor, arms plunged into icy water up to the elbows, they rubbed and scrubbed. Bon Papa, who always had time to spend when it came to her, took Catherine to see the Percheron draft horses at the market in Aigle. Another favorite goal of their walks was the tomb of the unknown soldier, where they stopped for several moments without exception . . . Bonne Maman had worked hard to see that the tomb was not moved. And each year, on the first of September, Bonne Maman and Catherine paid a visit to the grand Château of Villeray, overlooking the village. For Catherine, it was Sleeping Beauty's house.

Summer after summer, Catherine watched her grandmother sew and make jams. No one noticed that Catherine had grown. She took flight earlier than the other children—children, career, it all happened—but she would never forget the tender and inexhaustible love that had nourished her throughout her very short childhood.

"Something always brought me back to Villeray and nothing gave me greater pleasure. After Bonne Maman's death, my mother settled in her parents' winter house in the village. On the other side of the road lives Reine, her sister-in-law, a jolly soul who knits sixteen

159

hours a day behind her window and raises everyone's spirits. In this little village, where nothing ever changes, I feel at home."

When Catherine learned that the château she had visited in her childhood was for sale, she didn't even bother going to look at it. She would occupy this enormous house effortlessly, hardly touching a thing . . . as if she were returning home. Of course, nothing is ever exactly like before. Catherine's château is so vast that she can easily welcome her five children and eight grandchildren, offering them the supreme luxury of space. Camille, Marine and Bertrand, Louis, Victoire and Manon, Atlantique and Clara . . . the two youngest can leisurely chase each other in the endless hallways. They can play hide-and-seek in the alcoves, and gently open the carved wooden doors of the old provincial armoires where Catherine has organized piles of beautiful old sheets, damask tablecloths, and pillowcases hemmed with lace, between which are nestled little sachets filled with petals of vanishing scents. Nothing is exactly the same, but the spirit is there, the spirit that must have reigned at Bonne Maman's, a warm and gentle atmosphere, a shared tenderness at every moment.

"With my children, my grandchildren, and all our friends, the house is quickly filled," recounts Catherine. "We are rarely fewer than thirty on weekends. I have established a rule, a single one, but I hold fast to it: No one is to get up after ten o'clock, otherwise a gust of panic blows from the kitchen. In the summer, we eat under the trees. As I get the love of pretty things from Bonne Maman, that complicates life a bit. We set up several tables covered with baize. Then there are endless comings and goings with silverware, porcelain dishes, and embroidered napkins."

In winter, the tradition of these festive meals is carried on in the forest at the time of the hunt, around immense bonfires. There, also, the tablecloths fall to the ground grazing a thick carpet of leaves.

PRECEDING PAGES *Manon and Atlantique in the music room.* OPPOSITE *Everyone often gathers in the kitchen, which is furnished with pine furniture, for meals. In the pantry, Margaux prepares a cake for two young waiting gourmets. Faithful Jim clearly wants to be included in the party.*

ABOVE *In the old provincial armoires, piles of embroidered sheets, openwork tablecloths, initialed napkins, between which are nestled little sachets full of fragrant petals.* RIGHT *In the laundry room, one irons on a table, as in the past.*

Catherine has the baskets, candlesticks, and ancient carafes brought from the château. At night, they sometimes gather in the candlelit greenhouse. The children are always there, for Villeray belongs to them as well. It is only much later that they will go back to their pretty dormitories, where, well ordered behind the curtains of their little beds, eyelids finally closed, they will fall asleep, too tired for stories to be read to them.

It is then that Catherine, peace restored, pushes open the door of her room. Then, she approaches a window that looks out over the village. Down there, all the way at the bottom of the main street, she can make out the winter house. On this night, as on every other night, a light lit by her mother shines in the same place behind a window. A sign in the night, soft as a kiss, to say "until tomorrow."

OPPOSITE *On each floor, an immense corridor crosses the château.* ABOVE LEFT *View of a child's bedroom, with its campaign bed nestled in an alcove.* ABOVE *Little beds of iron and linen curtains: the monkish simplicity of the girls' dormitory.* OVERLEAF *The former orangery where, in autumn, Catherine gives her hunt dinners.* PAGES 170–171 *A walk among high trees leads Catherine's friends from the château of Villeray to the woods.*

167

HOLLY GROVE

ABOVE *Matthew tends a crowded poultry yard.*
OPPOSITE *Emma and Matthew were immediately seduced by the immense garden where Elizabeth and Kitty dine as soon as weather permits.*

With her parents and her numerous brothers and sisters, Emma lived in a Queen Anne house surrounded by a garden in the English style and an immense and generous orchard. Emma grew like a flower of the fields. A friend of plants, insects, and birds, she hated to see grasshoppers imprisoned in jelly jars or a blackbird in a cage. And she knew that ladybugs brought good luck. When one landed on her bare arm she would hold her breath and gently bend her elbow to give it more room to move about. Then she would watch it climb to the turned-up sleeve of her blue blouse.

In sandals or in boots, fair weather or rain, the children were sent outside "to breathe," television banished from their lives. Left to their own devices, they gave free rein to their imaginations, inventing endless games, day after day. One of their favorite occupations consisted of pretending. Pretending to be ponies, for example. The surroundings of the house were soon transformed in their eyes into an obstacle course. The whole gang began to leap over hoops planted in the lawn, bicycles, rakes, chaises longues, everything!

We are in the 1960s, and the adults were not having a bad time of it either. The time was welcoming, even exciting, the house always filled with friends. Emma's parents gave parties. They danced a lot. Head on her pillow, Emma let herself be transported to the shore of sleep by the carefree brouhaha that arose from the garden, accompanied at long intervals by the "clack" of a wooden mallet striking a croquet ball. One carries memories inside forever.

When Emma became a renowned potter and married Matthew, a

172

173

talented watercolorist, they lived in London. "We had 'an easy life,' with ~~height of luxuries~~ an office just steps away. All of a sudden, we became so absorbed in our work that we hardly ever saw our babies. Only during the weekend when we invaded the country houses of our friends with our two daughters, our dogs, and our baggage. In order to save a last small group of friends, Matthew and I decided that it was time to reverse the situation."

The house they found in Norfolk resembled, "a little less pretty perhaps," the one in which Emma had grown up. Located on the edge of a village, it is large enough to accommodate the family, their friends, their friends' children. And all dogs. Emma discovered the school, on the other side of the road, which seemed to have been built for dolls; Matthew saw the Victorian greenhouse—love at first

ABOVE *One barely leaves the stair before one is in the garden.* ABOVE RIGHT *For Emma, color expresses the joy of living. A map of the region was hung in the entry.* OPPOSITE *In the living room, with its walls covered in red felt, Elizabeth and Kitty inspect their treasure boxes.*

174

177

OPPOSITE AND ABOVE *At Holly Grove, books invade everything—the walls of the library, those of the studio where Emma creates her collections of ceramics and Matthew paints, and also the halls and stair landings.* LEFT *Beetle poses in the little salon.*

sight for both. Today vegetable and flower gardens abound. In a gigantic henhouse all kinds of cocks, turkeys, guinea fowl, geese, and several generations of rabbits, first adopted with enthusiasm by the girls and then fallen into disgrace, frolic amicably, pursuing their careers in absolute peace. In the courtyard await an antique Deux-Chevaux and an Austin, no less ancient, whose doors are decorated with wooden veneer, around which several extremely rare chickens forage, introduced to England by Emma's grandmother.

The welcome is warm in this kind of Noah's Ark that has not

178

known the Flood. One of the house's large rooms serves as a studio. Emma comes and goes, her new baby in her arms. Elizabeth and Kitty will soon be home from school and Matthew will return from London, where he goes twice a week on the seven o'clock train. "Matthew and I are totally aware of what our parents did for us. Yet, to try to reproduce the past would be unrealistic. Let us simply say that we are trying to reinvent everything, inspired by our memories."

The year is marked by important events. Just before Easter, the family sets off in search of nests fallen from the trees, which will be an important element of their table decorations. Elizabeth and Kitty will place inside chocolate eggs covered with white sugar, so beautifully made one would think they were real, while Emma will

179

get down from the shelves her collection of porcelain chickens, much tamer than those that scoot about outside. As soon as spring begins to flower, they choose a place in the garden—not too far from the kitchen—to set up an immense British Army tent. The smallest ray of sunshine is then a pretext to eat a meal outside, and only the harshest autumn chill ends the practice.

"Over the years, I notice the resemblances between yesterday and today, in the pleasure we feel in entertaining our friends or the way in which we send our girls to play in the garden as our parents did with us. We also have a room devoted to dressing up. And I also think I chose this house because Kitty could go to the village school on the other side of the road as I did."

To find the taste of childhood is one form of happiness.

Bibelots, souvenirs from trips, delicate cottons and antique shawls: Emma's bedroom is invaded by a happy disorder.

180

TIDEWATER

ABOVE AND OPPOSITE
*Tidewater evokes the houses
of the Old South.* BELOW
*Cally and her mother
together, like every summer.*

It is the peaceful hour. Seated in the depths of huge white
rattan chairs under the high columns of the veranda, Cally and Elie
slowly look around. The last rays of the sun still caress the waving
green slope that stops where the Cocheco and Piscataqua Rivers
join together at the foot of the fields. A red speck—a late flying
cardinal—flashes across the space between two majestic oaks.
Twilight settles in, erasing the details of the landscape. There is
an exquisite softness in the air. At long intervals, Cally and Elie
exchange several words in a low voice so as not to trouble the
silence that softly envelops them like a light coat.

A half hour from now, their always-numerous friends will join
them at Tidewater. The children, Anthony and the twins Caroline

182

and Alexander, will make their appearance several minutes before dinner, which will be held, as usual, around the mahogany table in the candlelit "big dining room."

Twenty years have passed this July since the birth of the twins and the discovery of Tidewater. This is perhaps the necessary time to create a true family house.

Of old American stock—she descends from the only baby born during the passage of the Mayflower—Cally wanted to come back each summer to New England, the land of her ancestors, where her parents had settled. She thought only of staying near them, for she did not want to break the very strong ties that bound her children to their grandparents.

As soon as she entered the colonial-style house that Captain

186

William Flagg had built for his beautiful Southern wife, Cally felt
that she was home. Elie had a pool built, restored a second building
for friends. He added wings to the body of their house, so perfectly
integrated with the old architecture that they seem to have been
there forever. Then they moved in to spend the first in a long dance
of happy summers.

The children quickly explored the house from top to bottom.
Each had his own bedroom, his own private territory. And soon the
tree house appeared, lodged in the welcoming branches of a
beautiful oak. "Their playroom was nestled under the roof," Cally
remembers, "and they created papier-mâché forts and aluminum foil
armor. We were happy and very close to one another, and the
thousand silly things we did enchanted us.

"When the house is full, we like to play charades or other such games after dinner. I always take the precaution of separating the twins, who can never be trusted when playing on the same side. But then, of course, they fight to be on the side of their grandmother— the cleverest of guessers."

Then there are moments, among the happiest, when one finds oneself without guests, alone with one's family. Cally remembers just one such August night when she and her husband fetched the twins from their beds. They went out with blankets and the half-asleep children to lie on the grass. One had Caroline, the other Alexander in the crook of an arm. For a long time they watched the shooting stars rain down and made wishes. "That was perfect happiness."

189

A BIRTHDAY IN THE COUNTRY

ABOVE AND OPPOSITE *The
presence of family furniture
gives rooms a unique feeling.*
BELOW *Peering in the gate.*

The drive makes a last curve around the pond where white
ducks are swimming and heads straight for the house, whose entry
is hidden behind a pretty iron portal. This autumn morning rings
with the deep barking of the "terrible" Ranulph, who gallops up to
meet a small group of bicycles returning from the market. The
willow baskets, hung on the rear, overflow with salads and fruits.
Pedaling without haste, the riders remark, as they pass by the old
pear trees, that they had better think, after lunch, of gathering the
fruits that have fallen to earth during the night and then of visiting
the walnut tree whose shells, still hermetically sealed yesterday, will
soon liberate brown nuts.

To the right of the house, set back from the drive, a former

192

Christmas tree has grown, a bit by accident, to majestic proportions. The beautiful balance of its branches, full of dark needles, elicits general admiration. On the other side, behind the linden trees and on a great expanse of lawn, a gingko biloba, a cedar, and a maple, whose leaves will soon transform into red flames ringed with gold, grow more slowly. Thérèse carefully chose the placement of each tree and watched them grow with the same eagerness with which she watched her three children.

For Thérèse and Armand-Ghislain, to have a house in the country brings a kind of authenticity to their lives that they do not find in the city. Le Haut Chaillot, an eighteenth-century house built on a piece of Armand-Ghislain's family's property, is not a place fixed in time—quite the opposite. Thérèse took a great pleasure in reuniting furniture and objects from different locations.

Today, her birthday is being celebrated on a fine September day. Lunch will be in the courtyard under the catalpas. Armand-Ghislain has returned from a meeting in town; the two eldest children, Alexis and Marguerite, who have been sleeping late, like most twenty-year-olds, have awakened. Félicité and her friends Victor and Alexandre, three true accomplices, are making beribboned packages in the upper salon. There will be not one, but two birthday cakes, crowned with candles. And memories abound.

The walks in the rain in the Encoeur woods when the children, having jumped in the ruts, returned with boots full of water. The expeditions across the fields in the heart of winter when black crows flew through the gray air and one kept up a good pace, cheeks frozen and hands stuffed into pockets, to hastily reach the house where steaming tea and cakes awaited. New Year's Day, when Thérèse digs out a thousand and one treasures from the cupboards to decorate the feast table. Twelfth Night, when—eyes bound—one of

OPPOSITE *A gallery of grandparents with severe countenances watches over Armand-Ghislain's office, the walls of which are paneled in pine. The stone staircase that leads to the salon was in the eighteenth century an exterior stair. It was enclosed many years later. The gun rack—now displaying canes—was made by one of the family's gamekeepers.*

195

the guests divides the cake and everyone chews carefully, hoping to find the hidden favor. And always, the return of birthdays and their shows, prepared by the smallest children in greatest secrecy with the enlightened aid of Nunu, in honor of the hero of the day.

Le Haut Chaillot is many more things as well. Armand-Ghislain, who tries every Sunday to lead his lazy flock to mass. Jean-Louis, his father, who wittily plies the art of conversation over coffee. So many things . . . not forgetting Faust, king of long-haired dachshunds and a great hunter if ever there was one, who in his younger days disappeared for entire hours to come back, totally filthy, to recover from his exertions on the loveliest armchair in the house.

Le Haut Chaillot, thanks to Armand-Ghislain, Thérèse, Alexis, Marguerite, and Félicité, has become a true family house.

ABOVE AND BELOW *Félicité carries in the birthday cake!* RIGHT *After lunch, the traditional walk in the Encoeur woods.* OPPOSITE *Victor and Alexandre enjoy themselves around the romantic pond planted with yellow iris.*

198

Personal Inspirations

They date from the seventeenth century, the eighteenth century, today. They are of wood, of stone, sometimes covered in plaster. They may be large or small. One finds them sheltered by a walled garden, nestled in the curve of a clearing, perched at the top of a hill.

Rustic or more sophisticated, they have one thing in common. Whatever their style, they always have something very resolved about them, as when one leads a thought to its conclusion, undoubtedly because they are the reflection of a dream. A dream that is transcribed into reality by a very personal vision of what a family house should be.

Each in its own way, these houses interpret the desire we have to be together, to create landmarks, to invent or perpetuate our family traditions. It is extraordinary to see the speed with which they recapture past times.

In all these family houses—and in spite of their differences—the givens are the same. They ask that we look on the following generations with the same indulgence and severity that was accorded to us. They ask for love.

Such is the spirit of these very different family houses, eternal as the turning of the earth.

LE COLOMBIER

ABOVE *Le Colombier beneath its carapace of red tile.*
BELOW AND OPPOSITE *A family walk.*

The house slumbers, enveloped in the pink cloak of dawn. It is at the far end of the village in a park enclosed by walls. Beyond, the meadows stretch out as far as the eye can see. It is not yet time for the boys to mount their bikes and head off on the country roads.

In the deep peace of dawn, Le Colombier has a truly proud demeanor under the shell of its enormous Burgundian roof of red tiles. Way in the back of the house, on the second floor perhaps, behind a door, one hears the sound of an alarm clock. With a kind of shudder, casement windows are thrown open. The kitchen is perfumed by bread and coffee. A new day begins.

Le Colombier is a dream that has become reality.

Franka did, in fact, dream of escaping Paris with Guy and their

204

OPPOSITE *Returning from school, the boys escape to the television room.* LEFT *Tom likes to work on the computer in Guy's office.* ABOVE *Tom watches for his father.*

ABOVE AND OPPOSITE *The great luxury of family houses is space. One loses oneself there in order to better find oneself again. Two good boys at bedtime, the twins Gaspard and Robinson.*

four sons. She dreamed of a true family life. For her, that meant the six of them all together, with dogs, cats, chickens, and a garden. That was her vision of happiness. They had no fixed ideas of a location in which to launch the dream. But, while crossing Burgundy to head south, they found Le Colombier.

For Franka, a true city dweller, this was a complete uprooting. She wasn't used to the country; yet, without apparent effort, she slipped into the rhythm of the days that passed. She had never had animals, except for Lux, the sheep dog she visited on vacations to her grandmother's when she was little. To live in the country changed everything. Today, Aïcha, the little cat, reigns over Le Colombier along with Youpi, a Scottish sheep dog, very large, very dependable, very affectionate, and who would be a lap dog if allowed.

Behind the orchard at Le Colombier is the vegetable garden,
where Franka made her first attempts as a gardener. As she gradually
grew bolder, the garden's borders widened and deepened. She
spends hours among the salad greens before returning to her kitchen
to spend hours more making sauces and jams. Guy tends the fires;
that is man's work. He tours the garden, notes the dead trees, cuts
the wood, and brings it in.

It is good inside when cold comes and one gets as close as possible
to the blazes that light the fireplaces. Guy and son Tom scrutinize
the screen of the computer; the twins Gaspard and Robinson have
started a construction game; Franka has taken a book from the shelf;
while Thill daydreams on the couch. They are together. They are
well. They are fortunate to live out their idea of happiness.

Scenes of everyday life: the salon and its fireplace of Burgundy stone, the kitchen where the heart of the house beats, the family at the market. OPPOSITE *Guy and Youpi on the balcony.*

HALF HOUSE, HALF GARDEN

On one side of the barn, Lee added a room where mosquito nets hung between the beams let the breeze pass through.

To have a house of one's own doesn't mean restoring the recent past but rather selecting the best for one's new family. Lee had decided that her house would be open all year long, that she would go there each weekend, that she would practice at leisure her talents as a gardener. This plan did not speak to her of Southampton, where she had spent her summers as a child in a house simply furnished with rattan furniture. This was a beach house, peopled in summer and closed in winter. Instead, she and her husband, Fritz, began to travel through New England, convinced that they would finally fall under the charm of a Greek Revival house. But the façades punctuated by tall white columns seemed too perfect to them, too pretty, as if they had come from the hands of a meticulous toy maker.

212

Discouraged, they almost decided to search elsewhere. Then one day they noticed a barn whose rustic and unpretentious appearance was agreeably out of tune with the area's polished style. "I loved the way it looked out over the valley. The landscape around it was just as I had imagined it in my dreams. I knew right away that we had reached our goal." Several months later, it was as if the barn had always been part of their life. It had taken on the somewhat bohemian look—half house, half garden—that we recognize today. Lee's garden tools very quickly gained ground, sliding even under the beds, just as the books of the bibliophile Fritz had before, nibbling up more and more space.

Lee had the idea of creating a large room, where walls would be replaced by immense screens stretched between the beams. This arbor-room, located on the side of the house, bathed at all hours by delicious breezes, is transformed into a kind of luminous ship at dusk, lit entirely by candles. Lee had been looking for a spot to bring in her potted plants, and so she had a large greenhouse built on the other side of the main house, where, in addition to her vases, her trowels, and her pruning shears, she placed a fireplace, a table, and chairs. "Dining in a jungle by the fireside in winter has a quirky quality that pleases me," explains Lee. "At Christmas, we put up the tree there. When our son Josh was little we used to go choose it together. It was a great excuse to argue. I always found it too small. Fritz, on the contrary, insisted that it was too big, while Josh got lost in the paths of the nursery. Back at the house, we decorated it from ladders that were never quite tall enough. I tried to convince Josh, with infinite diplomacy and not much success, to hang his favorite ornaments, which didn't correspond to the idea I had of 'my tree,' on the lower branches, but we always ended up agreeing that we had the prettiest Christmas tree in the world."

PRECEDING PAGES *In this room, a living room and kitchen at the same time, it is good to live around the Franklin stove, which converts into an open fire in the winter. On the floor, an early twentieth-century American hooked rug.* OPPOSITE *Off the master bedroom is a sleeping porch where one can capture summertime breezes.*

ABOVE *The house is entered through a large greenhouse where the family eats dinner in the winter in tropical splendor.* OPPOSITE *The garden's presence is everywhere, even in the summer bedroom, where tools are stored.* OVERLEAF *The barn made of pine appears buried in the garden.*

As Christmas approached, everyone began to hope for snow. Each one took his turn in the garden to sniff the air, scrutinize the sky, be on the lookout for the first flake. For snow added a magical dimension to the holiday. With it came silence and a sense of isolation that made the refuge of the house even more precious.

Each year is the same. The cat, Cheshire, prefers to remain in a warm place. Zoe, the dog, who would not miss the departure for midnight mass for anything, stands wagging her tail by the door. In the village, the church already reverberates with hymns. On Christmas morning, if it has snowed, the white expanse will be covered with a fine crackling film. In spots, one can sink down to one's knees. Lee, looking at her slumbering garden, will begin to think of spring.

 AMERICA IN FRANCE

ABOVE *Family photographs.*
BELOW *Bird housing.*
OPPOSITE *Her shingled house
reminds Françoise of the one
in which she was married in
East Hampton.*

The air is scented with roses and freshly mown grass. Standing in the clearing, Françoise, a slender silhouette, turns her back to the house, which seems to have come straight from an American dream. She is far off, lost in her thoughts. What is she thinking of while caressing the flowers with her gaze? Perhaps of the Chinese proverb that says, "One becomes a full human being if one has written a book, built a house, and made a garden."

Françoise's childhood was cradled between two family houses. The first, near the forest of Fontainebleau, had sheltered four generations: her great-grandmother, her grandfather, her mother— who watched Françoise grow up—and she and her sisters. In the eyes of the little girls it was a magical place, where treasures of photograph albums yellowed by time accumulated and which, at the end of August, smelled wonderfully of preserves that the cook stirred in immense copper basins.

The second house, belonging to a great-aunt, was in the Haut Doubs, almost on the Swiss border. "We went there as a family for shorter but, in our eyes, just as interesting periods. We whirled around in the kitchen like excited little flies, begging the grown-ups to let us peel vegetables and fruit. Sometimes, for the sake of peace, they gave in, which slowed them down a lot. Sealed in glass jars, conserves piled up one by one on the shelves of a room which seemed immense to me, a kind of back-kitchen designated solely for the preserved fruit of summer."

Sold and transformed, these houses disappeared from Françoise's life. Yet they still exist in the form of crystal-clear memories, moments of intense happiness that she, along with Philippe, also orphaned from his family house, wanted to pass on to their four children.

OPPOSITE, TOP *The kitchen, decorated with Italian ceramic tiles and marble, is separated from the dining room by a bar.* OPPOSITE, BOTTOM *Françoise at the stove. Over the sideboard, the portrait of an eighteenth-century gourmet.* ABOVE *On the dining room side, an English oak restaurant table surrounded by Windsor chairs. Behind is a Shaker-style cabinet. On the wall, a series of hand-colored engravings representing fruits found in Normandy.*

225

ABOVE *The living room is treated like the rest of the house—a cameo of beiges and whites. The sofa and its collection of cushions are lit by two lamps designed by Christian Liaigre. In the center of the library wall, a painting by Michael Weston.* OPPOSITE *Sober harmony in the bedroom where Françoise's desk of bleached oak and woven raffia rests against a pine wall painted white.*

Their goal was to create an atmosphere rather than to restore the past. Françoise had dreamed of returning to the Haut Doubs; Philippe thought of the Southwest, his region. After hours and days of discussions, they called a final truce and opted for Normandy. They decided to build a wooden house—which made Françoise think of her cabins in the forest and the farms of the Jura, and Philippe of American landscapes. The children insisted on an attic, Philippe a study in which to write, and Françoise made plans for a vast kitchen–dining room so they would always be together, with a back-kitchen filled with preserves and jams as in the Haut Doubs. Once finished, they took possession of the place with the impression that they had known it forever. Indeed, this was the case since houses are the reflection of what we are.

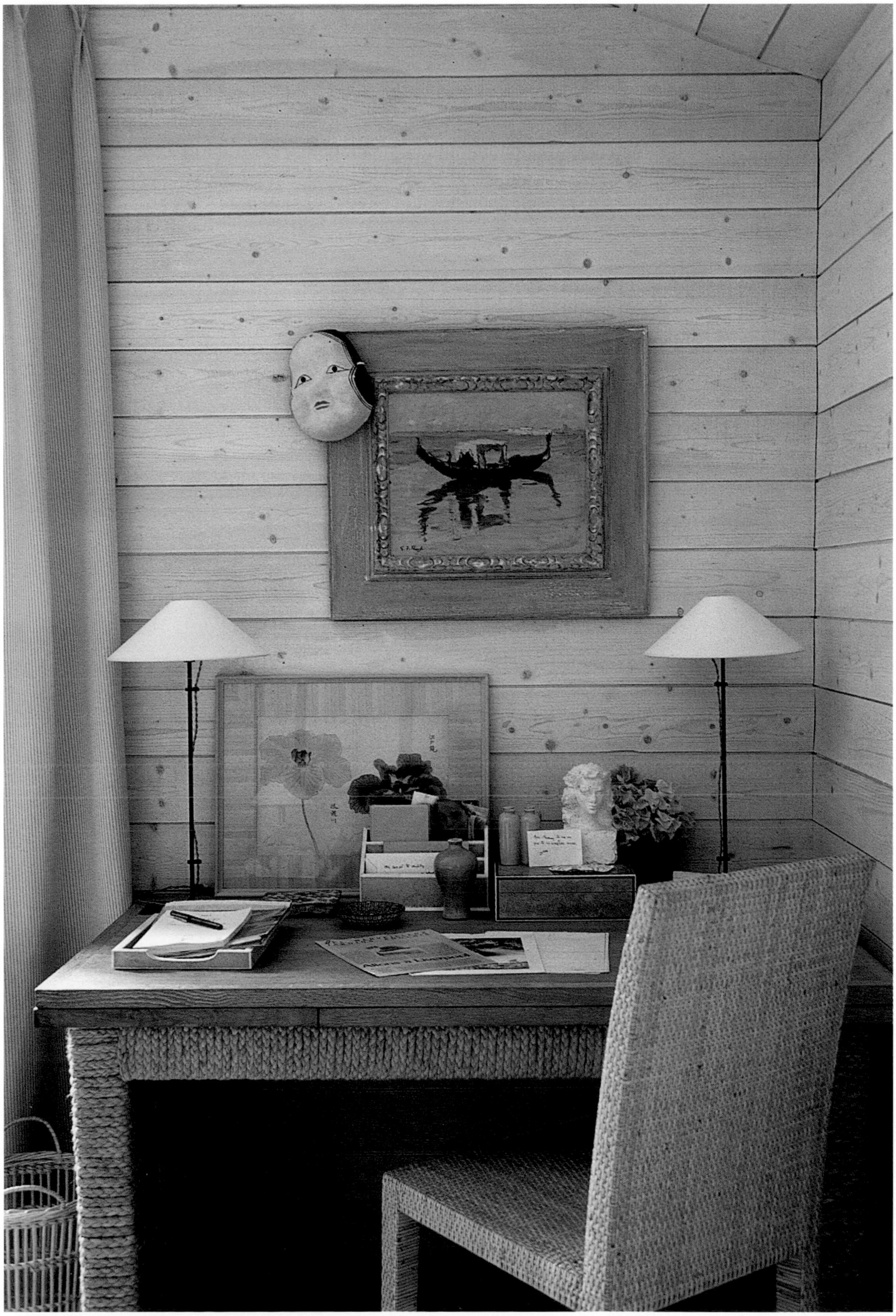

GOING BACK HOME

*Backed up against the road,
Rouchaudy is a former farm
that in summertime
disappears under roses,
honeysuckle, and clematis.*

Marie-France, on her father's side, is of pure Aveyronnais stock, and following the traditions of this very poor region, her great-grandparents came to Paris to make their fortune. They may have left behind them the family house in Laguiole, but that didn't mean that they had abandoned it. Distance only fanned the flames of their desire to return, which they did each year, with good weather. Marie-France's grandmother, having raised three children by herself and having wisely increased the family fortune, returned to Laguiole each summer, preceded by her trunks and surrounded by her daughters to greet her only son, his wife, their six daughters, and their two little sons. "That made a lot of people, not counting the cousins scattered about the area.

228

"The house, spread out lengthwise as is typical of the region, was an old farm with a stable and a barn, which over time had taken on a kind of bourgeois fullness. It was a very gentle universe, over which my grandmother kept watch like a queen—an essentially feminine universe, where my father, until the arrival of the boys, was the sole representative of the masculine tribe. My grandmother occupied one part of the house, we occupied the other, but we lived together. On the second floor, the very simple children's rooms opened onto a long hallway. We slept two by two, in narrow beds. Even in summer, the nights were cool and we slid with delight under our bedcovers, to renew in the silent darkness the threads of our whisperings, interrupted by the arrival of day.

"We often went on picnics, with rarely fewer than twenty

OPPOSITE *In the old days, one-fourth of the house was devoted to living and the rest to the farm, with a cathedral-like barn above and a stable below. Up to three families often lived behind the walls of thick basalt and granite blocks.* ABOVE *The sweetness of life: a cup of tea in the verdant gardens.*

231

RIGHT *The half-light of the salon is made more poignant by the waxed oak furniture, a sofa and armchairs covered in brown velvet.* BELOW *Because of the snakes, young and old never leave for a walk without a cane or a stick.* OVERLEAF *In winter in this harsh and poor countryside, one remained seated in the imposing fireplace on two benches, the cantons, while soup simmered over glowing coals.*

ABOVE AND OPPOSITE *In the kitchen–dining room located in the former stable, Marie-France wanted the brightness of traditionally whitewashed beams and vanilla-colored wainscoting. A large English counter divides the room in two, and the Regency table is big enough to fit Bernard and Marie-France's large family. In the English dresser, a collection of faïence.*

people, for our numerous cousins were added to these expeditions. We set off loaded down with willow baskets full of tableware, glasses, pâtés, salads, cakes, and fruit. As soon as we found the ideal location, we spread large tablecloths out on the grass and unpacked our thousand and one treats. If we had stopped by a stream, we children went fishing for crayfish. Once, on one of these long hikes, we stopped at a shepherd's hut where the shepherds who stayed there five months to keep their animals in the open fields prepared an *aligo* for us, this delicious purée of potatoes with Cantal cheese. We were cut off from the city, on another planet, perfectly happy."

Like all children, when rain began to beat against the windows, Marie-France and her sisters disappeared into the immense attic, which covered the entire length of the house. "At the top of the

236

stairs was a room full of funerary wreaths which frightened us. This
did not stop us from cracking open the door each time we passed.
Just the opposite . . . just to savor the great frisson that would run
through us." The little girls then hurried to the spot where the
trunks were stored and, to the deafening tattoo of the downpour that
echoed on the roof, draped themselves with old fabrics, tried on
huge capes, and pinched their waists into the corsets of long ago.

After dinner, Marie-France's grandmother liked to conjure her
childhood. She told stories of the region, stories of her arrival in
Paris. The assembled group played chess. Some, under the luminous
halo of the lamps, embroidered pillowslips. Their father was always
ecstatic when he saw his girls doing handwork.

"Our parents looked after us. We grew up under the shelter of

237

their love, without hurrying. When we became adults, we put off as long as possible the time when we would have to leave the house at Laguiole."

Marie-France and Dominique, the inseparable eldest, barely moved away from each other at all. Each summer, like their grandmother before them, they both escape Paris to seek shelter in the arms of their childhood, to inhale again the smell of new-mown hay, of flowers, of the sun, and of warm cinders in fireplaces so deep that one could stand upright. Today, it is they who receive their children and grandchildren, who gather roses in the garden, who tell stories. The roles have changed. It is they, today, who teach the youngest the treasures of tenderness and impart to them, for it is their turn, all the great and all the tiny secrets of happiness.

CHEZ MONINA

The road weaves between pools of sun and shadow. It is one of those discreet roads, almost a bit turned in on itself, that never really seem to lead anywhere. But then there is a little stone house at the center of a large clearing, in the shadow of a beautiful and very old tree, a house that resembles a child's drawing—Monina's.

Monina and Edward rented in Bucks County for a long time, moving from one place to another, each time leaving memories and regrets. One day, they said to themselves that they felt like always coming back to the same place with their children.

When she took the little road for the first time, Monina felt her heart beat. It beat even faster when she saw the house standing in an island of greenery. She saw, of course, that the tree had been planted

It is a stone house at the center of a large clearing, in the shadow of a beautiful tree.

242

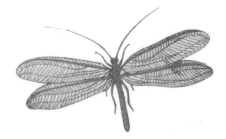

much too close to the entry, but she said to herself that it would be good to be in the shade in summer. The façade, pierced by symmetrical openings, pleased her. She imagined, right away, one of the two little abandoned gardens, overflowing with weeds and scarcely enclosed by the traces of a fence, transformed into a potager. The other would collapse under peonies.

It was love at first sight. Edward succumbed in turn. They each knew that at the beginning of a love affair one sees things with rose-colored glasses. The good, and even more often bad, surprises come later. If one can overcome the latter, there is a chance that the love affair will last for life. Monina and Edward did not overlook this rule, which holds true for houses as well.

Deceptively charming, the house leaned dangerously, as if

ABOVE *In the kitchen, on the dining room side. Against the back wall, an American eighteenth-century country sideboard, which Monina decorated with lace after a trip to Brittany.* OPPOSITE *On the painted and sanded paneling, a collection of paintings brought back from all over.*

LEFT *One feels comfortable chatting in the kitchen while leaning on the Pennsylvania-style table or seated in the English armchair covered with a Russian fabric from the thirties. Behind the stove, the wall is covered with delft tiles.* ABOVE *Lunch in the shelter of a porch roof.*

ABOVE *The mantelpiece, from a Lancaster County tavern, is decorated with delft tiles; above it, a maplewood sculpture by Christopher Hewitt.* OPPOSITE *A nineteenth-century sofa covered in petit point, under an English seventeenth-century still-life.*

suffering from extreme fatigue. In one bedroom, Monina resorted to slipping telephone books under the feet of the bed on the left side, lest the designated sleeper spend an athletic night scaling the mattress. Serious work was needed to put the house straight.

In the living room, which occupies the complete width of the house, were two fireplaces. How fortunate, they thought. Then came one of those freezing nights when one likes to take refuge by a fire. The family gathered around the master of ceremonies, attentive, a bit anxious as always when one lights a fire for the first time in a fireplace one doesn't know well. Edward struck a first match. The logs began to crackle and everyone congratulated themselves—for ten seconds—for it didn't take any longer than that for the second fireplace to begin to spit forth torrents of smoke!

ABOVE *Opposite the
American eighteenth-century
maple four-poster, an
eighteenth-century chest of
drawers in the same wood.*
OPPOSITE, LEFT *A corner for
washing up.* OPPOSITE, RIGHT
One of Monina's bouquets.

"We had quite a few little domestic adventures like that one,"
recalls Monina. "The house had no real kitchen. Meals were
prepared on a part of the porch which was more or less isolated from
the house by bay windows. Each winter the dishwasher froze and
my feet were like ice cubes."

After building a new kitchen, after having devoted a long time
hunched over cans of paint searching for the exact shade, having
spent hours scraping, sanding, and nailing, Monina looked at her
little house and said that she was happy and decided it was high time
to take the time to watch her plants grow. One becomes attached to
a house when one has suffered for it to make it prettier, more
comfortable. It is, then, a reflection of oneself.

Monina loves to feel the caress of seasons. In winter, she loves

that there is nothing particular to do. Often, the garden is engulfed by snow. One hears only silence. In springtime, one sees her thin profile passing back and forth in a flight of multicolored petticoats. Her arms are filled with flowers.

In summer, the heat is leaden. There comes a time when the thick foliage of the tree no longer protects the house. One moves about very little. The walls take on humidity. They have to be wiped down several times a day. Though there is birdhousing made by the local carpenter, one independent family prefers to settle under the veranda. These birds, a family in the larger sense of the word, with cousins, little nephews, nephews' friends and friends of friends, are very happy, very noisy, they have many children. They, too, know that Monina's house is a good home.

251

The porch, at the back of the
house, evokes peace and the
sweetness of life.